# Alignment for Success

## Bringing Out the Best in Yourself, Your Teams, and Your Company

### KATHARINE HALPIN

ISBN: 069228723X
ISBN 13: 9780692287231
Library of Congress Control Number: 2014916036
The Halpin Companies, Inc., Phoenix, AZ (AH 9/5/14)

# About Katharine Halpin's Work

"Thanks to our conversations over these five years, I have more time on my calendar for real rejuvenation and am a more strategic leader. Even more importantly, we have laid a very strong foundation for the future so that Blue Cross Blue Shield of Arizona will have continued success, even in the midst of health care reform."

**Richard Boals**
**President & CEO**
**Blue Cross Blue Shield of Arizona**

"Thanks to Katharine, my teams are stronger because I learned to communicate my expectations more effectively. Key team members have enjoyed the opportunity to contribute and be recognized for their contributions."

**John Buchanan**
**Partner, PricewaterhouseCoopers**

"Katharine has been a friend but even more, an executive coach and mentor to me and a number of members of my executive team. She brings enthusiasm and energy to everyone she meets. As a result of our work with her, we now have the right leaders in the right roles."

**Linda Hunt**
**Sr. Vice President of Operations, Arizona**
**Dignity Health**

"You wonder if anybody can really make a difference. We found that Katharine was able to do that. She encourages everybody to speak honestly and directly with each other without getting into a fistfight."

**Herman Orcutt**
**Founding Partner, The Orcutt Winslow Partnership**

"With Katharine's coaching, I dramatically improved both my style of communication and my relationship with targeted professional associates. Her coaching has profoundly changed each person and the organization itself. Organizations will find that Katharine's work will dramatically improve their results and create a fun, integrity-based culture."

**Valerie Manning**
**CEO, Greater Phoenix Chamber of Commerce**

"You have helped the team take the meaning of personal accountability to the next level. You have a wonderful ability to help leaders grow from the inside out."

**Carol Poore**
**Vice Provost for Institutional Advancement, ASU West**

"Prior to my work with you, our company was successful and growing. However, at times we were chaotic: miscommunications popped up way too often, and project margins were not meeting goals. Also, some of our employees were not as productive as I wanted them to be. When I met you, Katharine, I assumed our only option was to upgrade our staff. You, however, taught me how to communicate my expectations to our staff in a positive and clear manner. Understanding my expectations gave them the opportunity to rise to the new challenges. A few people did choose to 'opt out' and left the company. But, by communicating differently, the rest improved tremendously. Everyone is a lot happier, because they know where they stand. Clear communications had another positive effect:

new people we attracted were superior performers and better team players."

**Eric McDowell**
**Partner, The McDowell Group**

"After working with you for only 60 days, I am pleased to report that my company has experienced record revenue and profit. Additionally, all of my key players have demonstrated even more initiative, accountability, and commitment to our company's success. Lastly, I am sleeping better at night because I have a very short 'to do' list."

**Tim Kinney**
**President, Kinney Construction Services**

"WOW! Our work with you allowed us to get the most important issues out on the table. Your tools then helped us get these issues fully resolved within 60 days. With your support, I have strengthened my ability to be a strategic leader within the firm. Thank you for the behind the scenes role you are playing in our success."

**Daniel G. Bruce**
**Partner, Baxter, Bruce, and Sullivan P.C.**

"You presented invaluable methods to align our business plan with priorities and day-to-day activities, taught us how to increase effectiveness in driving execution and decision making based on the facts, and helped to increase both the comfort level and effectiveness around conducting candid, authentic, constructive, inclusive dialogue with grace and graciousness."

**Paul Luna**
**President, Valley of the Sun United Way**

"I wanted clarity, and with your help, I got it real fast. Today I know what to do, and I know better how to get there."

**Sheila Grinell**
**Founding President & CEO, Arizona Science Center**

"The quantum-leap results that we generated for our organization allowed us to generate revenue that did not require any reduction in our staff through either attrition or layoffs."

**Sally Shreve**
**Area Vice President, Silicon Valley High Tech Company**

"You have been wowing our members with your seminars since 1997. You are a bankable commodity and sure-fire crowd pleaser who delivers practical, timely information. Here are a few recent quotes:

- I learned more about myself in two hours than I have in the past 2 years.
- Excellent, excellent, excellent!
- Katharine has many practical ideas and tips and is inspiring in many ways as well."

**Cindy Natani**
**Director of Marketing & Public Relations,**
**Arizona Society of CPAs**

"Our Arizona Chapter of the Institute of Management Consultants rated you a whopping 95% on delivery and 98% on content! The group hears more than twelve speakers annually and can be very jaded. You, however, knocked their socks off. Everyone loved your interactive format. They took as many notes as possible. They laughed. Your method of getting them involved, providing usable content, and having fun was refreshing and outstanding."

**Bill Blades, CMC, CPS**
**President, IMC Arizona Chapter**

*"Be yourself; no base imitator of another, but your best self… Listen to the inward voice and bravely obey that.  Do the things at which you are great, not what you were never made for."*

RALPH WALDO EMERSON

# Contents

The stories shared in this book are true. Names and environments have been changed to protect the anonymity of our clients and business colleagues.

# Preface

WE FACE A crisis in the workplace. Leaders at all levels are ill-prepared to articulate, even to themselves, which ideas and actions are most strategic, critical, even feasible to execute. Workers are exhausted by the expectation that they will be available electronically at all hours. As a result, few are thinking clearly. Even fewer are executing effectively. Everyone operates under significant stress and intensity which will eventually affect their mental and physical health. Arianna Huffington eloquently summarized our current environment in an interview in *Science of the Mind Magazine*:

> "The Western workplace culture – exported to many other parts of the world – is fueled by stress, sleep deprivation and burnout. Even as stress undermines our health, the sleep deprivation so many of us experience in striving to get ahead at work is profoundly and negatively affecting our creativity, our productivity and our decision making."

*Alignment for Success* provides simple, practical, easily-implemented solutions to these challenges. Regardless of how many years experience you have or the rank you hold in your company, you will gain immediate and tangible benefits from this book. Change comes from the top down, but the pressure for change can also work its way from the bottom up. While *Alignment for Success* expressly targets CEOs, their C-level team members, and Boards of Directors, frontline workers can also embrace these concepts. These principles and tools will support anyone on a quest to work in a high-performing organization.

**Who will benefit from *Alignment for Success?***
- Executives and managers.
- Leaders and aspiring leaders at all levels, from the mailroom to the boardroom.
- Entrepreneurs and small business owners who want to increase the value of their companies quickly.
- Trainers, teachers, professors, coaches, and consultants.
- Students in business school programs.
- Everyone who wants to accomplish results by bringing out the best in others.

A leader in a high-performing organization embraces the need for alignment. Alignment does not just mean everyone nodding their heads in agreement. Alignment means that every person understands three important points:
- The vision and purpose for the entire organization.
- The current goals for their team to achieve the vision.
- How their activities fulfill the vision on a daily basis.

How do you get alignment? First, the tone is set at the top. A commitment to self-leadership at the top of the organization builds alignment. Next, honest communication builds alignment by nurturing conversations that get the right people into the right roles doing the right things on a daily basis. This is why *Alignment for Success* opens with self-leadership practices you can begin today. Then, it continues by demonstrating the communication skills you need to build alignment throughout your team. *Alignment for Success* closes with ways you can take this newfound alignment to the whole organization, everywhere you go.

### *Alignment for Success* teaches you to:

- Communicate clearly and effectively a compelling vision that engages everyone.
- Negotiate expectations through a well-constructed plan of action.
- Create trust and credibility by modeling the behaviors you want to see.
- Coax others to speak honestly, with candor, and stay engaged in important conversations.
- Create win/win resolutions that dissolve, not just resolve, conflict.

Are you ready to get started?

# Acknowledgments

I WISH TO thank all those that helped me achieve this milestone:

All the strong women in my family and community who invested so much in my development; my grandmothers, my aunts and my mentors, Faye Rutland Lancaster and Hazel Lominick Milner.

My unique and free-spirited parents, John F. Halpin, III and Mary Lou Halpin, who shared with me their love of people, stories and laughter. They were the biggest influences in my life and career and taught me the importance of creating inclusive environments where everyone felt heard, validated, and appreciated.

My life-long teachers, my siblings: Harley Halpin Caldwell, John F. Halpin, IV, Will Halpin, and Lucy Halpin DeRossette.

My spouse of almost 35 years, Bonnie Meyer, who has created the space every day for me to bring my best self to my life and my work.

My Coach U community including Susan Corbett Klein, Cindy Reinhardt, Dan McNeill, Judy Sabah, Sandy Vilas, and our very own rock star, Cheryl Richardson, who taught my first Business Builder class.

Key colleagues including Karen Ussery, K. Sue Redman, Jamie Millar, Beth Jarman, PhD, George Land, PhD, Vickie Champion, Tammy Holmes, Maureen Webster, Sarah Schantz, Coni Bourin, Mary Gendron, PhD, Nelda Majors, and Karen Bailey.

The Halpin Companies Team: Barbara Ralston, Jeanine L'Ecuyer, Vikki Scarafiotti, Janis Keeley, Deborah Bateman, and Deb Peck, PhD.

My Mastermind Group of Allan Milham, Maggie Hunts, and Michelle May, MD.

The late Bill Johnson and his MMG Group.

The Book Team of Betty Rauch, Lois Zachary, PhD, and Matthew Howard.

Each and every client who has given me the privilege of serving as their strategic thinking partner since 1995.

# Introduction

## Katharine's Story

LIKE BEAUTY, LOVE and art, we all think we know leadership when we see it. But do we? Judging by recent economic downturns, along with ethical and moral lapses that make front-page headlines, true leadership is in short supply today.

From the time I was eight years old, I spent Saturday mornings with my dad at his accounting firm's office. There, he would share stories that fascinated me. Not many little girls would find accounting enthralling, but I did – especially the "people" side of the business. Dad would share stories about his clients, their companies, their involvement in the community, and their employees. Dad always focused more on the people than their financial statements and tax returns. I trace my passion for creating workplaces that work for everyone back to those memorable Saturday mornings.

Years later, while studying accounting at the University of Southern Mississippi, I still worked in Dad's office. But then, instead of having a child's fascination with it all, I felt like an indentured servant. My dad had an expectation that my primary focus, even during high school and college, would be his CPA firm. As a result,

I started having a conversation in my head that made me believe I was responsible for everything at home, at work, and in my life. My belief was if something were to be accomplished, it would be because I rolled up my sleeves and did it.

I escaped my crazy home environment to work at the Dallas office of a "Big 8" international accounting firm. With no awareness of how deeply my early life had affected me, I brought my own dysfunction to a work culture fraught with competing agendas, poor communication, and outright sabotage. Most of my colleagues coped with this environment by following the old cliché of "go along to get along." Some people were rewarded and promoted. Others quit. I began to develop an endlessly looping conversation in my head – one that always started out with, "My boss is an idiot." Soon, I found myself ostracized and eventually forced out by that boss. Unfortunately, I had no awareness of the role I had played in that challenging situation.

For the next thirteen years, all my professional experiences followed the same pattern, despite the diversity of firms and industries where I worked. Rarely did I have the experience of working in what I call a high-performing organization, one where I could flourish. Not only was I choosing workplaces where I would inevitably struggle. I was also poorly suited for any kind of detailed analysis. I am a people person. Not having any awareness of my real strengths and not having worked in environments that encouraged me, I never focused my strengths appropriately. As a result, I constantly found myself in the wrong roles. All I managed to accomplish was alienating my employers.

In 1993, for the third time in ten years, I received an offer for a very generous severance package. I was a hard worker, smart, and took more initiative than most employees. I had received accolades for the ownership I took and the long hours I worked. So, why would companies be so willing to compensate me to go away? I believe the reason they were so intent on moving me out was that they sensed my lack of authenticity. My early life had led me to develop negative attitudes and beliefs, and overly critical judgments of others. I had become an inauthentic person.

Anytime I felt the slightest discomfort in a meeting, I would launch into a very loud, obnoxious, and disruptive conversation in my own head about my direct supervisor. On the outside, I could say to my boss, "That's a great idea." But in my head, I always finished that sentence with, "You idiot!" And though I only said it in my head that negativity may as well have been a flashing neon sign on my forehead. Surely the people around me sensed my negative judgments and poor opinions.

I see now that working in the unappreciative environment of my dad's firm had fostered within me a desperate need to get credit - to be perceived, even by myself, as the most dedicated person in the room. When a person's strengths are not recognized and appreciated, when they do not feel they have a voice in decisions, they can spiral downwards into neediness. I did that in spades. I was my own worst enemy.

After I had accumulated enough severance packages to wallpaper my office, I had to admit that the common denominator in all these encounters was me. With a tremendous amount of self-examination, I developed an awareness of the triggers that would cause these conversations in my head: overwhelm from volunteering for too many tough assignments, fatigue from working long hours, inconsistent time for reflection, and a lack of consistent exercise. When I stopped going to the gym, I started making up even more stories in my head. All of this made me hypersensitive. If I felt the slightest indication that I would not get the recognition and rewards I felt I deserved, I would launch into my internal tirade. Eventually, I realized these knee-jerk reactions did nothing but hand over control of my career to someone else, time and time again.

Just as my career and health were both careening over a cliff, I discovered the field of professional coaching. I began my journey of personal growth with coach training at Coach U. This training laid the foundation for my transformation from an unsuccessful CPA into to an Executive Coach. From there, I grew as a facilitator of large-scale initiatives to build work environments where everyone is encouraged, engaged and empowered. Now, senior executives all over the world use our proven methodology and tools on a daily basis.

The founder of the profession, Thomas Leonard, introduced me to professional coaching in 1995, and I hired my first coach based on his recommendation. With the help of my Coach U community, I learned how to stop myself from reacting inappropriately by simply taking a few deep breaths. I learned to leave my office and get outside in nature during the workday. I learned to get energy from healthy activities like exercise and gardening instead of the sleazy energy generated from feeling superior to my boss. I stopped working 60-plus hours a week so fatigue would not cloud my perspective. I learned that I could look at situations from a broader perspective when I practiced self-care. I learned to examine my own role in my conflicts and how I had contributed to the chaos. In short, I began to learn self-leadership!

I worked on self-leadership until I could become a role model for others. Soon, my own clients started to apply these same practices. These methods empowered them to reach their full potential as leaders.

Twenty-plus years later, I can see I was born with some innate talents and strengths. I have an ability to see the big picture. I have a commitment to making work environments more productive and positive for everyone. I have the ability to naturally and intuitively bring out the best in others. I can create a sense of safety that results in transparency for all. My career problems, rooted in my early work history with my Dad, were exacerbated because I never took positions aligned with my natural strengths and abilities.

Therefore, I have dedicated my life to helping leaders create transparent, communicative environments where people's roles align with their strengths. This alignment generates extraordinary performance, productivity, and profit. My clients report that they make more money, have greater peace of mind, and can now help others do the same. Seeing revenues and profits increase by 200 to 300 percent is normal for our clients, and these high-performing environments benefit leaders and teams from the boiler room to the boardroom.

Experience has taught me that one basic factor makes all the difference between a low-performing workplace infected with mistrust, and a high-performance workplace where people creatively collaborate to solve problems: self-leadership. That realization led me to write *Alignment for Success*. This book promotes self-leadership tools anyone can use to create a culture in which people deliver consistent, predictable performance, far greater productivity, and a profitability that delights stakeholders at all levels.

*Alignment for Success* provides a practical handbook with proven, step-by-step tools for building corporate cultures that tap into basic human needs for honesty, respect, and appreciation. With this book, leaders can easily develop their own self-leadership capacity and then build transparency and alignment at the individual, team, and organizational levels. It has been a long journey to this point for me, but I couldn't be happier to share it with you now.

## CHAPTER 1

# Unaligned:
# The High Cost of Chaos and Fear

**WHAT IS ALIGNMENT?** Alignment comes when our actions express our values. Aligning our actions with our values requires playing the right role on our team. When we have the right people in the right roles doing the right things, our organization becomes fully aligned. A company with such strong alignment will achieve its vision.

Leaders begin to create alignment when they first align their own actions and values. This self-alignment grows naturally out of the practices of self-leadership discussed in *Alignment for Success*. By becoming a role model for alignment, the leader inspires and invites others to become aligned. With the self-awareness and communication skills covered in *Alignment for Success*, leaders actively develop alignment throughout their entire company.

To understand the importance of alignment, we will look first at some examples of companies that did not have it. These companies struggled with chaos, fear-based decision making, and poor performance. Next, we will explore how the practices of *Alignment for Success* brought clarity, transparency, engagement, and empowerment to similar organizations. We will take you step-by-step through a proven methodology that will unlock the potential of alignment to drive the success of a high-performing team.

## The High Cost of Chaos

The CFO is often the first to recognize the high cost of chaos. It does not appear as a line item in the financial statements. But, a CFO recognizes the warning signs. Performance, productivity, and profit fall below expectations. Rick McPartlin, co-founder and CEO of The Revenue Game, believes the cost of chaos runs as high as 30 percent of gross revenue in many organizations. Chaos means confusion: both individual confusion about what we are trying to accomplish, and team-wide disasters when people are confused about how we will accomplish it.

Consider a well-known rental car company in Las Vegas that risked losing major market share because of customer complaints. Despite having once earned an extraordinary customer satisfaction ranking, they now suffered from constant operational breakdowns that led to unhappy customers. The teams responsible for running the company smoothly on a daily basis no longer responded in a timely manner. Their ability to confront and solve problems had degenerated into a chaotic mess where nothing seemed to get fixed or go right for very long.

What had gone wrong? The company had recently promoted a long-time employee. She had a reputation for building great teams and producing extraordinary results. But now, her Operations Manager noticed she was so protective of her new team that she failed to hold them accountable to the company's high performance standards. She made excuses for their errors, treating each break-down as an isolated event. Her protectiveness led to isolating her team from the rest of the company, preventing any collaborative partnerships with other managers in her region. The Operations Manager, in frustration, planned to request a transfer for her to a back-office division. But even then, the tidal wave of existing problems would have to be confronted.

When we began consulting with the Operations Manager at the troubled rental car company, we found two major drivers of chaos. First, we found a superstar in an inappropriate role – a role not aligned with her values and her strengths. Her reputation for building great teams, we discovered, was very much aligned with her whirlwind of energy and enthusiasm for launching new projects and initiatives. The routine of managing daily operations really gave her no outlet for the drive and passion she brought to gathering a group of people together and rallying them around a common cause. As a result of being promoted into the wrong role, her unhappiness with the basic functions of her new job had begun to drag down her entire team, taking the company's profitability with it. Secondly, we discovered a significant lack of alignment throughout her team. Just like their leader, individual team members had taken positions not really aligned with their values and strengths either. These workers turned out to be highly capable people, shoe-horned into positions in the company that made them look like poor performers.

The chaos of this department was costing the company profits in terms of happy customers, but also the loss of productivity caused by stressful and ineffective workplaces. If only all companies in similar circumstances could reduce these costs of chaos, we could turn around our economy in short order. Instead of paying for re-work, unproductive teams, lost customers, and high turnover, companies would have funds available for capital investments, expansion, and new jobs. Chaos is a major source of friction in the engines of our economy. Before we lay out a plan for reducing chaos, however, let us look at another company with a different but just as costly problem: fear.

## The High Cost of Fear

Fear is a powerful emotion. When we are afraid, our fear can override our ability to think and act rationally or reasonably. The fear begins to permeate every decision we make.

Companies and workplaces face many fears: fear of not meeting Wall Street's earnings expectations, fear of losing market share to competitors, fear of taking too much or too little risk, fear about inadequate resources, fear about other people's expectations and competing priorities, fear of the clock running out before all the work is finished on a project. Fear even permeates the boardroom, especially when the Board of Directors finds itself confronting sensitive matters. Even when their past experiences warn them of danger, they can remain silent for fear of making the wrong decision, or fear of offending others on sensitive topics. Discussions in such an environment remain superficial, and sometimes the Board passes the buck by deferring to management. In fear-based conversations, we avoid genuinely sharing our deepest concerns in ways that let everyone else be fully heard, too. This is why fear is the enemy of transparency and alignment.

To fully understand the high cost of fear, consider a major telecom company that launched the latest version of their smart phone in the mid-2000s. Outwardly, they received accolades in the press for their breakthrough technology. But inside the organization, the engineers knew the software contained a major glitch. They had tried and failed to get the attention of management, to gain time and resources to address this glitch before the product went to market.

Management, however, insisted on timing the product launch to coincide with their quarterly earnings report to the investor community and Wall Street. Their fear of not meeting expectations clouded their perspective. Their mindset could not be changed, even when confronted with the facts by the engineers - the experts on the technology. For lack of a productive and genuine conversation about how to resolve the engineering concerns, the product launched on its intended date, with the glitch unresolved.

When the new phone hit the market, customers soon learned their calls would drop off randomly, regardless of proximity to a cell tower. A sophisticated, multi-national customer complained first. Their executives were early adopters of new technologies and had been excited to get their hands on this latest device. 5,000 executives turned in their old phones and activated the new, faulty phones. The massive volume of calls from this wave of irate executives flooded the telecom's IT department and customer service lines.

The telecom company exacerbated the problem with a directive to its Customer Care technicians to deny any knowledge of the glitch. Each customer, therefore, was treated as an isolated incident. These first customers met a wall of denial instead of a team that gave a voice to their common complaints in a unified way. The angry customers soon took their complaints public via social media channels. You can imagine the public relations disaster that ensued.

The press quickly picked up on the controversy. In another communications misfire, the CEO appeared at a hastily-assembled press conference that ended with a temper tantrum and foul language instead of answers to the tough questions. A video posted online shortly thereafter went viral within hours. The stock price plunged to an all-time low. Management got their wish to have the product launch coincide with the quarterly earnings report – but with disastrous consequences.

Who was to blame? Engineering blamed marketing for rushing the product release. Marketing blamed engineering for inadequate testing. Management bought into the finger pointing and blamed everyone but themselves. But, the real enemy was fear. While all of these teams knew about the problem before the release, no one had the courage to take a stand and force a later release date. Fear had created an environment where people could not honestly voice the nature of the problem nor collaborate to solve the problem. Fear had degraded all discussion of the problem until no one could be heard.

To stop that sort of toxic cycle, we must drive out fear. To drive out fear we must encourage and welcome every idea, concern, and challenge to the status quo. We must ensure that everyone feels free to speak up. We need organizations where people believe that their voice will be heard, places where people know that any concern or problem will be vigorously addressed – not swept under the rug. Without this environment, fear spreads like a cancer, killing performance and profits in the process.

Alignment is the key to driving out this fear, to reducing the high costs of both fear and chaos. The journey to alignment throughout an organization begins with the leader. Letting go of fear requires self-leadership. Self-leadership is a practice that develops the self-awareness, authenticity, and honest communication required to facilitate inclusive discussions that address everyone's fears. To create an environment where others feel safe to speak up, leaders must first open themselves to others' ideas and concerns, to respect other people's perspectives. In the next chapter of *Alignment for Success*, we will begin that journey of self-leadership.

## CHAPTER 2

# Self-leadership: Aligning Your Own Actions

BILL GEORGE, THE former CEO of Medtronics and now a Harvard Business School professor, often shares in his books and articles about leadership failures. The common thread in Professor George's stories is that when leaders fail, it is not because they failed to be a leader to their people. Instead, they failed to be a leader to *themselves*. Strategic leadership of a team or organization requires being a leader to yourself, first and foremost. So, what is self-leadership, and how do we build this foundation?

Self-leadership consists of a few simple practices and habits that enable you to manage yourself, your time, and your life. I attribute the success of my firm to these simple habits and practices. You have read about the first half of my career where I was not successful. Now let me share the habits that have laid the foundation for the success we have enjoyed at The Halpin Companies since 1995.

## Pace and Intensity

The most common challenge to adopting any new practices in life is finding the time to implement them. Leaders often get so caught up in activity that making time to adopt new practices just does not happen. Why is this? I believe we suffer from what I call the "drive-focused approach." A desire to be the driving force leads us into situations where we must be constantly on the go. We have developed an idea that we need to be high-energy movers and shakers, but we confront the trap of rushing through things, and doing too many things at once. The really important things in our daily life get brushed aside so we can take care of the really urgent things. Our pace and intensity traps us in dealing with a stack of things that need to be done right now, while neglecting the fundamentals we need to address to become fully aligned.

We can see this effect most clearly in the value our culture places on multi-tasking: doing many things all at once. But what happens when we multi-task? We lose focus. The distractions of juggling phone calls, emails, face-to-face conversations, and putting out random fires on a daily basis begin to degrade our effectiveness at dealing with any one of those things.

Studies now show that the ability to multi-task is a myth. Our brains are not wired to multi-task. Dr. David Meyer, Director of the Brain Cognition and Action Laboratory at the University of Michigan is a mathematical psychologist and cognitive scientist who received his Ph.D. from the University of Michigan. In Sue Shellenbarger's *Wall Street Journal* article *Multitasking Makes You Stupid*, Dr. Meyer says,

> "People who are multitasking too much experience various warning signs. Short-term memory problems can be one. Intense multitasking can induce a stress response, an adrenaline rush that when prolonged can damage cells that form new memory... Other red flags are changes in your ability to concentrate or gaps in your attentiveness."

In other words, if you try to read through your emails while talking on the phone, you will have a harder time remembering any of the information from either one of them. This memory damage has more serious long-term effects than merely getting lost in a phone call, however.

The frantic and frazzled leader caught up in a whirlwind of multi-tasking will lack the reflective self-awareness required to build alignment and transparency in their organization. Without self-awareness, we will nod our heads in agreement when people talk, but we won't really be listening. We will appear to be in alignment with them, but then proceed immediately to sabotage our efforts and our team by demonstrating detrimental behaviors or taking contradictory actions.

How frantic have your own days become? Honestly answer the seven questions in the following assessment to determine where you are today.

| THE FRANTIC AND FRAZZLED ASSESSMENT | | | |
|---|---|---|---|
| For each question, select the response below that best describes how you feel today. | | | |
| Do I... | Daily | Sometimes | Seldom |
| 1. Have more time than I need? | | | |
| 2. Arrive early? | | | |
| 3. Block at least one-hour of unbooked time? | | | |

| | | | |
|---|---|---|---|
| 4. Use a "Planner Pad" or other system to manage commitments made by other people to me – and by me to other people? | | | |
| 5. Record everything on paper or in an electronic format that is easily retrievable? | | | |
| 6. Prioritize and allocate resources effectively? | | | |
| 7. Have time to think strategically? | | | |

Scoring: Give yourself 10 points for each Daily,
5 for each Sometimes, and 0 for each Seldom.

**60 - 70**: You are most likely a self-motivated peak performer who is organized, focused and grounded. You plan business and personal commitments in advance so one does not impede the other, while leaving room for the unexpected. As a result, you consistently respond effectively at any given moment, and can adapt to your circumstances as needed.

**50 -59**: You are most likely a high performer who often balances day-to-day business and personal commitments efficiently. You often plan these commitments in advance and are relatively centered. However, without consistent white space on your calendar, unexpected obstacles and "fire drills" will reduce your personal and professional effectiveness.

**30 -49**: You are most likely an average performer who manages business and personal commitments as they come. Your sporadic enthusiasm to plan ahead and anticipate unexpected obstacles demonstrates inconsistency in your performance and effectiveness. Sometimes you deliver on time and on point, while other times you find yourself in the midst of chaos and confusion, missing commitments as well as opportunities.

**29 or Below**: You are most likely an under-achiever due to a low degree of focus or lack of knowledge on how to increase your effectiveness through managing your time and yourself. Inability to manage your time results in missed commitments and opportunities, to the extent that others tend not to count on you to follow-up, follow-through or deliver on your promises. You often find yourself in frenetic situations both on and off the job. You often feel overwhelmed, but you most likely do not realize it is self-imposed.

## Think Time

How do we stop this cycle of frenzied activity that blocks our self-awareness and reduces our effectiveness? The first step is scheduling time for introspection and structured reflection, what I call "think time." In this think time, we clarify our vision, examine our roles and actions, and reflect on our values – all key components of becoming truly aligned.

As leaders, we must often live extroverted lives. Taking quiet time to pause and reflect may not come naturally to us at first. Why do we focus on what seems like an introverted practice? Because a leader must first be self-aware in a way that leads to awareness about their teams, their colleagues, and the challenges they face. Only with this higher level of awareness can they enter into the honest communication that will build alignment throughout the organization. If our pace remains frantic, we will miss the nuances of the situation. Awareness includes the ability to sense what is *not* said as well as comprehending the full meaning of what *is* said.

In order to gain this heightened sense of awareness, we must pace ourselves. Drive and intensity may have us rushing from one meeting to the next. The intensity of our thoughts prevents us from distinguishing facts from stories, reactions from responses, and the biases inherent in our own perspectives compared to others. Pacing of our own thoughts requires a structured approach to self-leadership, and that structure begins with think time.

Think time requires sitting alone, undisturbed and unplugged from the media, with nothing more than a pen or pencil and a blank pad of paper. Schedule this time for an hour each and every week and hold yourself to taking this time. Most often, the results our clients experience prompt them to schedule even more think time, as often as every day.

During think time, ask yourself thoughtful questions. In *How Did That Happen*, Roger Connors and Tom Smith, write that a "better, more effective question" than "how did that happen?" is "how did I let that happen?" In your daily or weekly think time, you can take each situation and dissect it. Think through the original objectives and the desired outcomes. Reflect on the current situation and the gap between what you have and what you want. Identify questions you might ask to get the project back on track. *Alignment for Success* includes, at the end of this and each remaining chapter, Questions for Your Think Time that will make good starting points for you.

Understanding relies on clarity. When we bring the specific details of our current situation into focus, we can often see a pattern or a trend. If a negative outcome happens over and over with the same person, for example, we might see a pattern that illuminates the root cause of these negative outcomes. Too often we rationalize someone's poor performance by saying, "That's just the way that person is." Ask yourself questions like, "My colleague has a problem working with Client XYZ, but isn't this situation very similar to the problem that arose when he worked with Client ABC?"

Now you can begin to discern a pattern. With this new awareness of the pattern, you can easily grasp some of the potential root causes. Perhaps your colleague will never be effective in a role that requires negotiating with a client or customer. Maybe he lacks the necessary interpersonal skills to manage relationships. Or, perhaps the company does not have enough structures to help your colleague prepare for and be successful in these circumstances.

Regardless of your ideas about the root cause, you can now craft some questions for your colleague. Developing an ability to ask the right questions of a situation is one of the most important gifts of the practice of think time. Here are some examples of questions you might raise with your colleague:

- Do you have any thoughts on the cause of the current situation?
- Have you been juggling too many projects?
- Do you have enough time to prepare before your client meetings?
- Would it be helpful if I helped you prep for these meetings or even attended some with you periodically?

- How might I help you in getting better prepared to meet with clients and negotiate the specifics of these client engagements?
- Do you think this situation has any similarities to the situation that arose last summer with Client ABC?
- Could you see yourself taking some think time to reflect and see if there is a pattern or a trend? And if so, what is the root cause?
- Could you take that think time by Thursday so you and I could meet again on Friday to brainstorm solutions to this root cause?

Think time is one kind of time we need to schedule for ourselves regularly. I call these "reserves of time." A reserve of time is a space on your calendar during your workday where you get to catch your breath. It is a support structure to stop chaotic, frenzied activity and restore your focused perspective. Using these reserves of time empowers you to make good choices and solid decisions. They create an environment for you to have greater awareness and confidence so that you can use effective communication.

A reserve of think time before all of your meetings will immediately begin transforming your effectiveness in those meetings. Start small with this block of think time. Clear your calendar for twenty minutes between meetings. These small breaks help you fully prepare for each meeting. By eliminating the frenzied rush between meetings, you calm yourself down to where you can be more articulate, facilitating the honest communication that builds alignment.

In your think time prior to a meeting, carefully review what commitments you have made to the others at this meeting. What did you promise to deliver this time? Consistently asking this question will develop a better record of promises made during meetings. Review the purpose of the meeting. What do we need to decide, design, or discuss in the meeting? This empowers you to think strategically about the purpose, which you can then articulate at the beginning of that meeting.

This focus on purpose turns aimless meetings into productive meetings where you and your team understand the desired outcomes and their roles in delivering them. Your colleagues will be very pleased to have this information up front. If they know the purpose of the meeting is to simply get a briefing from you, they can relax and absorb the information being shared. If they know your role in the meeting is to get briefed by them so you can make a collective decision by the end of the meeting, they will be more focused. If they know your role is the sole decision-maker on the topic, they will understand this is their last opportunity to persuade and influence you to their recommendations.

Taking think time before a meeting seems like such a simple idea. But, I see otherwise very smart and capable people attending unnecessary meetings every single day, meetings where little gets done and few understand what the point of it was. Taking think time before meetings is just as important a reserve of time as the more reflective think time we must schedule for ourselves weekly or even daily.

If you need some help getting started on asking yourself the right kinds of questions during your pre-meeting reserve of time, begin with some or all of these examples:

- What exactly is the purpose of this meeting – planning, reporting, brainstorming, or decision-making?
- Are we at the right stage of this process to have this meeting now?

- Who will be the facilitator during this meeting? Are they properly prepared?
- Who are the required parties that should attend? Are these the same people who were invited? Who is missing? Who can be excused?
- What is my role to play in the meeting?
- Should we review our Charter at the beginning of the meeting so we all know our purpose and scope of authority?
- Do we have a well-thought-out agenda that all the participants have seen in advance? Should we take time at the beginning of the meeting to review the agenda?
- What outcomes do we need to deliver by the end of the meeting?
- By when should the work of this committee be accomplished?
- Who will be responsible for circulating the notes and plan of action?
- What kind of leadership does this group need? How can I prepare to bring that kind of leadership to this meeting?

On the one hand, it may seem tough to budget the extra time required to answer questions like these before all your meetings. On the other hand, when you start thinking strategically and making your current meetings more effective, you will eliminate all kinds of unnecessary meetings. When your meetings begin to clarify the vision and everyone's accountabilities, you will need fewer meetings to keep projects on track. You will spend less time "putting out fires" for your teams when your meetings begin to give them the clarity they need to work effectively and solve their own problems.

Most of our clients find that simply by taking an hour of think time weekly, they freed up another two to three hours each week. Is it not surprising that by slowing our frantic pace down to a more calm and effective one, we actually accomplish more than when we felt we were working so terribly hard? By observing the practice of think time consistently, our clients have freed up whole days on their calendar on a regular basis. When we stop running for our life on the hamster wheel of drive-focused, frenzied activity, we begin to work smarter, not harder.

## The Power in Patterns

When we give ourselves this gift of time, we start to notice patterns and trends in our lives. We sometimes see how our attitudes and expectations have been the common denominator in all the challenges we face. Without an ability to articulate our expectations to ourselves, we cannot negotiate those expectations with others. Without an ability to properly assess our attitude, we remain unaware of the unconscious but key influences in our ability to communicate effectively. When we have needs that have not been articulated to ourselves or others, we risk becoming irrational in our attempts to get those needs met.

Once we have an awareness of the role we have played, we can prepare to speak authentically yet do so in a supportive, collaborative, transparent way. When we know what we want, we can ask people for help. We do not leave people guessing. We say it up front, and we can say it with generosity and graciousness. This approach fosters genuine dialogue, not defensiveness.

Because leaders often work with great urgency and a very intense focus, they risk missing subtle clues about the nature of the problems they need to solve. When leaders slow down and build think time into their program of self-leadership, these clues become obvious. We begin to notice patterns and warning signs that should have told us what was wrong six hours ago, six days ago, or six years ago.

But, patterns do more than make it clear what the problem is. They also present solutions. When a leader schedules regular think time, she prepares her mind to spot the opportunities present in her challenges. She prepares herself to collaborate effectively with her team to capture these opportunities. And in terms of alignment, think time brings us to a greater awareness of who the right people are for the right roles to reach the right goals for the organization.

**Clarifying the Vision**
Bill Breen's article *The Clear Leader* quotes Marcus Buckingham, author of *First Break All the Rules*, on the importance of a clear, strong vision for the future:

> "There's something unique and different that makes a leader, and it's not about creativity or courage or integrity. As important as they are, you can have those attributes and still fail to be a great leader. A leader's job is to rally people toward a better future. Leaders can't help but change the present because the present isn't good enough. They succeed only when they find a way to make people excited by and confident in what comes next. The future calls to leaders in a voice they can't drown out. The future is more real than the present; it compels them to act."

In an organization in total alignment, all the actions of all the people align with the company's vision every day. In our opening chapter on chaos and fear, we saw what happens in companies that lack alignment with the vision. Without commitment to a clear, compelling vision for themselves, their people, and their organization, leaders fall victim to the vagaries of the economy, the challenges of rapidly changing trends, or the crisis of the day. Without a clear, compelling vision, teams struggle with conflicting messages that lead to inconsistent performance and unpredictable results.

In think time, we renew this all-important vision and clarify it in our minds. Our reflective time helps us really get a handle on the meaning of the vision, what it would look and feel like in action, and who are the right people to help us achieve it. This reflective time gives us an opportunity to literally visualize our colleagues' experiences as we fulfill this vision. That is what alignment looks like.

## Consistently Communicating the Vision

But, a leader must do more than simply know the vision. Leaders bear the responsibility for communicating that vision in everything they do, everywhere they go, to all their people. The leader's ability to consistently champion the cause of the vision is what we mean by consistency.

Consistency cures the diseases of chaos and fear that plague companies today. The clarity of vision achieved in think time prepares a leader to take a consistent message to the whole organization, a message focused on clear expectations with well-defined goals. When our people understand what they are doing, why they are doing it, and how we will measure their success, they will begin to bring their best selves to work to meet those goals.

Even previously dysfunctional teammates will transform themselves in order to meet clear expectations set around a compelling vision. The superstars on the team will shine even more brightly as they begin aligning their activities with the organization's purpose and goals. Rather than contributing to chaos and confusion, they will channel their high energy and boundless creativity in the right direction. Most importantly, the other 80 percent of the team will take their own performance to a higher level that will drive innovation, collaboration, profitability, and success.

Many leaders rely on tips in the most recent *New York Times* best-selling business book. While constant improvement is valuable, leaders who perpetually bring in the latest and greatest hot new formula for success run a terrible risk. An endless barrage of new approaches often causes chaos, because it makes the leader's messages inconsistent. Rather than offering their teams a consistent and compelling vision, they produce random messages confusing people and sending them careening in different directions.

A team that lacks clarity of purpose and the context that our values provide will eventually just put their own spin on such a stream of random messages. They hear the inconsistency. They sense the lack of clarity. They resort to making up their own stories about what the leader really means. And in the end, people on the team will take action not based on the true vision, but on their own *interpretations*. Chaos reigns. Fear seizes the day. Productivity and profits plummet.

For an organization to achieve total alignment, it needs leaders who can consistently communicate the vision and consistently demonstrate the behaviors that express that vision. Leaders develop this level of clarity about their vision in their think time. In the next few chapters of *Alignment for Success*, we will explore the communication skills that empower you to communicate it.

## Self-care

Self-care is fundamental to self-awareness and self-leadership. Without self-care we cannot remember our vision or our strategies, instead becoming immersed in random activities and unstrategic tactics. Self-care means different things to different people. For some, it revolves around nutrition and simple habits like eating an apple every day. For others, their program of self-care focuses on aerobic exercise and raising their heart rate. Exercise releases endorphins in the brain that give people more mental clarity and a more balanced perspective.

Most people include some form of spiritual sustenance in their program of self-care. They know that spending time in nature or in prayer and meditation brings out the best in them. In every spiritual tradition, mystics had their mystical experiences while in nature: on top of a mountain, under a tree, sitting by a river. Being in nature grounds us in the sense that we are part of something bigger than our selves. Time in nature provides perspective and allows us to not take ourselves so seriously. Sometimes, we can merge the spiritual and the physical through practices like yoga and Tai Chi.

If you are like most people, you might establish a goal involving exercise. You might know you need to make your goal measureable if you want to achieve it. And, you might even set the bar low to make it easy to achieve; for example, going to the gym two or three days every week. But this approach often fails, and we all have made New Year's resolutions that we never really carried out.

Why is that? The problem with the goal of doing a habit three times a week is that it does not provide enough momentum to build a long-term habit. Plus, if your goal is only three times, and you miss one because of unforeseen circumstances, you only get to the gym twice. That is no way to build a long-term practice. To make matters worse, many people get no satisfaction or joy from going to the gym. It is only another job or task for them on their list of things they have to do.

While I would never tell anyone to stop working out, I do suggest that you put some serious thought – and even some experimentation – into finding other forms of exercise that really do bring you joy. It might be something like joining a volleyball team or a dance class, if you prefer social activities. Or, if you prefer quieter time to yourself, you might schedule a daily yoga routine in the privacy of your home. Whatever choices you make, I encourage you to establish a goal of doing these energizing activities five to seven times each week. This results in enough momentum that if you do miss a day, you do not lose momentum over a period of several days. This is how you develop strong habits that give you energy and make you feel invigorated.

Each person's self-care program will be unique to them. There is no right or wrong way to do self-care. The objective is to experiment and find the habits that give you the most joy and the most satisfaction. This sense of joy and satisfaction is exactly what we want to build throughout your entire organization. It is the subjective feeling of total alignment. And, it starts with you.

**Questions for Your Think Time**

What activities do I wish I had time for because they are fun and bring me joy? What would it take to put some of these activities into place every day?

What barriers will keep me from achieving my goals of self-care? How can I manage this by tracking measurable progress?

In one or two sentences, what is my personal vision for my life? What are the core values I have that this vision expresses? Is everything I am currently doing aligned with that vision?

What is the vision of my team? Would everyone on the team agree with my answer? What do we do on a daily basis as a team to achieve this vision?

Who on my team knows exactly what their purpose is and excels at achieving it? Who seems confused about what their purpose is?

Can I think of any ways I am inconsistent or sending mixed signals about the vision and purpose of our team? What can I do to be more consistent when I communicate?

**Call to Action**

I commit to take the following action steps by this date_____
in order to build a strong foundation of self-leadership in my actions.
I am doing these things not just for myself, but so I can bring my
best self to my loved ones, my team, and my community.

1. _____

2. _____

3. _____

# Self-leadership: Aligning Your Own Attitudes

IN THE PREVIOUS chapter, we looked at think time as a concrete action we can take to begin aligning our actions with our vision and values. In this chapter we look at something a little less concrete but no less important: our attitudes. In many ways, attitudes are even more important. They will determine our actions by influencing the choices we make, the ways we handle other people, and our entire demeanor. Our attitudes about a situation and the people involved, and even our attitudes about our self, will color our perspective. I call these incredibly influential attitudes our "way of being."

Our way of being is comprised of our beliefs, judgments, and opinions. Self-leadership involves managing these judgments and beliefs. When we fail to manage our way of being, we risk communicating to others our judgmental attitude, putting them on the defensive instead of making them feel empowered.

When things go wrong, the first question to ask your self is, "Who was I being?" Who were you being that allowed your team to miss deadlines and expectations? Who were you being that encouraged people to disengage? People tend to live up to our expectations or live down to them. The choice is ours, and it is rooted in our way of being. To bring out the best in others, we need to demonstrate self-leadership in managing our way of being effectively and powerfully.

## Gratitude

Gratitude equals great attitude. Gratitude keeps you in the driver seat. A victim mindset puts others in the driver's seat of your life and your career. The question is: how quickly can you shift out of the victim attitude we often find ourselves in during any given day? Gratitude will shift your attitude instantaneously.

Self-leadership requires developing a sense of gratitude for your situation, your opportunities, your people, and your success. Even when things seem chaotic and success appears impossible, a leader refuses to fall into the attitude of a victim. Refusing to be a victim requires a leader to get absolutely clear about all the ways that their people add value to the team, the customers, and the entire organization.

When we find ourselves in conflict with another person, it becomes especially important to maintain this sense of gratitude about them and their contributions. When you find yourself facing unexpected distractions and challenges, remain grateful for them. After all, in the midst of a breakdown we find opportunities. Focusing on these contributions and opportunities takes you out of a reactionary, victim mindset and into a productive, proactive mindset.

When you have clarity about these gifts and opportunities, you can much more easily create an experience where others feel respected. This experience of respect builds trust and transparency at every encounter instead of conflict. You will find that you cannot sustain a negative or judgmental demeanor when you stay focused on how others add value. It is impossible to be in both a reactive mode and a proactive mode simultaneously.

We must come from the perspective of what is working instead of what is not working, and remembering the value of each person on our team. By making this attitude a part of our company culture, we foster connection and collaboration company-wide. When people have strong personal and professional connections, they will resolve conflicts quickly with much less drama, trauma, and chaos. But without a strong connection, no amount of negotiating will truly resolve conflict. Because it is so important to have our people in alignment instead of in conflict, we will share with you a practice that has worked wonders for our clients. It can transform your organization, too. It is called acknowledgment.

## Celebrating Successes

Alignment throughout an organization begins with what is working. It begins with recognition of individuals, teams, and whole divisions for their successes. Recognize a janitor who designed a better method of cleaning floors. Celebrate a data entry clerk who designed a new data field to increase productivity for a whole division. Acknowledge – in genuine, heartfelt ways – others and their specific contributions. When we celebrate these successes, we do more than just build alignment. We also identify successes we can replicate in the future. When we celebrate what works, and discover ways to replicate it, we lay the foundation for truly transformative levels of productivity.

The key to a workplace where others are encouraged, engaged, and empowered is to begin your conversations with acknowledgments.

Human beings need to feel valued, appreciated, respected, and included. These needs are basic and fundamental – just like our needs for food, water, and air. Beginning conversations in a way that meets these needs up front removes the defensiveness people can feel when dealing with conflicts or challenges. And, when you have a receptive, cooperative audience who trusts you, you can stay in the conversation and build much stronger alignment.

How is acknowledgment different from a compliment? It must be based on *facts*, not your *opinion*. Compliments are typically based on our opinion. If you simply share your opinion, someone might say, "Oh, I was just doing my job." They might attribute your positive comments to you as a matter of taste. After all, it is just your opinion.

Acknowledgments, on the other hand, include a specific explanation of how what they have done for you, another person, or the organization, has made a difference. When someone gets specific and measureable details about exactly what they did, it shows them you were paying attention. It shows them you understand the value of what they do. It shows them that they matter. This kind of specific feedback helps them internalize the positive message and leaves them feeling energized, engaged, and empowered.

When you acknowledge a colleague, especially in a team meeting with others, they feel even more than valued and appreciated. Public recognition helps them feel like a part of something bigger than themselves. This new awareness causes them to take more ownership and initiative, be more focused on results, provide more leadership, communicate more effectively, and be more loyal. We all need team members with these characteristics. It is not so difficult to hit the pause button on a regular basis and share acknowledgments.

I encourage you to begin your meetings and conversations with what I call "acknowledgments to celebrate success" as your first agenda item. This is an informal time where a leader and the team acknowledge where each other has succeeded recently. Everyone has the opportunity to identify some specific actions another person or a team took – actions that directly contribute to the success of the team. Some team members cannot do their job with total effectiveness unless someone else does an important job first. We can take time to recognize those that support our success and empower our own efforts.

What are the tangible benefits for a team when you share acknowledgments in a meeting like this? The primary benefit is the reinforcement of expectations and standards. When you acknowledge a high performer, it makes everyone else want to achieve that same level of success so they can be acknowledged too. Everyone steps up! This allows everyone to see what is possible for them as both individual contributors and as a team of high performers. You plant a seed for them, creating a vision for themselves and the team. You start to instill in your team members the desire to replicate and leverage this success. Lastly, and most importantly, you start to build more trust and confidence among the team members. They will naturally feel safer and more secure.

Once teams discover the energizing power of celebrating each other's successes through acknowledgments, the organization's culture experiences a transformation. As everyone learns to pause and share acknowledgments before pushing on to the next task or challenge, we begin to see a reduction in chaos and frenzy. Our people begin to find themselves in a reflective state, individually and collectively, where they can connect the dots and see the patterns. We discussed the power of patterns in our chapter on think time. Now, just imagine if everyone on your team had a chance to gain the same insight into trends, opportunities, and the team's potential. Imagine how many more problems your team could solve on their own if they gained this level of clarity about their operations on a daily basis. This is called leveraging success: your success, and the organization's success. When you start to replicate successes, these successes become greater in scope and magnitude. It is like success takes on a life of its own to become an integral part of your company culture. Alignment naturally begins to occur.

Self-leadership requires the great attitude of gratitude for this very reason. Once we manage our attitude to become more grateful, we sweep away the negativity that blinds us to the real value that people on our teams contribute every day, in large ways and small. By shifting our attitude, we become leaders who can acknowledge others for the specific contributions they make to the team. When we master this aspect of self-leadership, we can transform our conversations using acknowledgments to celebrate success. This builds a culture based on trust, honest communication, clarity about the facts instead of stories and opinions, and a commitment to everyone winning. You will find this approach far more effective than any intensity-driven push to force results. You will even find that acknowledging your people will bring far more successful results than pursuing recognition for yourself. This is how aligning your attitudes eventually becomes alignment for your entire organization.

## Instilling Personal Responsibility

The tone is set at the top! If your company has a culture of blaming, finger-pointing, defending poor decisions, justifying errors, and duplicating efforts, then the place to look for the source of these problems is in the mirror. If a leader blames their people for the company's lack of success, then the team members will go on the defensive, justifying and rationalizing their own poor performance. Sadly, this is human nature. This is the child in elementary school sheepishly reporting to his teacher, "The dog ate my homework." What do we gain from having a culture of defensiveness and rationalizations? Nothing.

Instead, we need to build a culture of personal responsibility, and that requires accountability. What is accountability? Over the years as a facilitator to leadership teams, I have often referred to *The Oz Principle* by Roger Connors, Tom Smith, and Craig Hickman. These authors have challenged me to ask our clients, "What else can you do to rise above your circumstances and achieve the results you really want?" These authors define accountability as "a process of 'seeing it, owning it, solving it, and doing it.'" It requires a level of ownership that includes making, keeping, and proactively answering for personal commitments. It is a perspective that embraces both current and future efforts rather than reactive and historical explanations.

Personal responsibility is holding yourself accountable: taking ownership of the reasons why something works – or does not work. How can we practice better self-leadership by developing this attitude of personal responsibility in ourselves, first? If you can enter a reflective mode for even a few minutes, just like you do in think time, you can often identify the role you played in a conflict or unsatisfactory situation. Let me suggest a short list of questions that focuses on what role we might have played in creating what we perceive as the problem.

- How clear was I on what I needed from the very start?
- How effectively did I communicate those expectations to the team?

- Did I put enough effort into securing their commitment to fulfilling those expectations, or did I just assume they were on the same page as me?
- Did everyone have a chance to articulate all their concerns during the planning stages so we could anticipate future stumbling blocks?
- Did I encourage even the most hesitant team member to speak up with questions and concerns?
- Does the team have the right people in the right roles based on their strengths and abilities?
- Do the team members have a clear commitment to the team success on this project? How do I know how committed they are?
- Does everyone on the team have all the resources they need to succeed? If not, how could I have helped them get those resources?

When we have too intense a pace, when we work in frantic mode, we often overlook our own failure to consistently communicate a compelling vision, articulate our specific expectations, or provide enough support structures for our teams to succeed. Personal responsibility entails taking 100 percent accountability when things go wrong. This attitude asks, "Who was I being that allowed this to happen?"

There are typically a thousand places where we could have articulated our expectations more clearly, first to ourselves and then to our colleagues. There are dozens of opportunities in every situation to communicate more clearly and more fully. When we find these missed opportunities, we need to own them. We need to be able to go to our colleagues or our teams and say, "I am so sorry. Now I see how I was not clear. I can see how I have not given you the level of support you needed on this project. I am going to do whatever it takes to get you that support. Can we get started right now with a clear vision and a plan of action?"

This approach to taking 100 percent accountability for the success of your team may feel strange at first. But if we are unwilling to model personal responsibility for our teams, who else is there? How can we expect our teams to align with the vision and take responsibility for achieving it if we have not shown them the way to do that? For good or bad, the tone is set at the top.

## React or Respond?

Reactions are a reflex. That is why we so often hear the phrase "knee-jerk reaction." Someone touches a nerve, and we react instantly without even thinking. What is the problem with this way of being? First, it takes all the control of the situation away from you and places it squarely in the hands of whoever can hit that nerve. Second, highly-charged emotional reactions can generate storms of negativity. The resulting arguments and hurt feelings can take far more time to resolve than the original problem at hand. They can also spread negativity throughout the organization in terms of gossip, resentment, and intentionally blocking the efforts of others at work.

Self-leadership requires us to respond instead of react. A response, unlike a reaction, is managed. In a situation where you could react instantaneously in a negative way, you may choose to instead respond in a productive manner. When you have enough awareness to catch yourself and coach yourself to respond, you have to the opportunity to craft an answer that honors your values and aligns with the vision so others may clearly understand. To understand how we put that concept into practice as part of our journey of self-leadership, let me tell you a story about Sharon.

Sharon was ready to walk away from her twenty-six-year career and six-figure pension. Her compensation had dropped by almost $200,000 for the fiscal year because of her colleague, Dan. Sales in their division had plummeted, and Sharon blamed Dan completely. Sharon came to me for coaching. At first, she wanted help dealing with this person she held responsible for the failure. In a loud, angry voice, Sharon told me all about how upper management was to blame for deciding to bring in an inexperienced executive from outside the company. She and her peers had all worked their way up from the bottom. And then, this outsider came along and brought down the whole team.

How much does that sound like the blaming that went on in the telecom company who released the smartphone too soon in the first chapter? Sharon held on so firmly to this attitude of blaming Dan that she – along with two other leaders in her division who felt the same way – had hired an attorney to file suit over the lost compensation. I could see that Sharon was well on her way to a very unhappy ending to her story if we did not exercise some fundamental self-leadership practices.

From what she told me about her career, I could see she was quite dedicated and successful. So, I began by acknowledging her for giving twenty-six years of hard work to the company. I acknowledged her dedication in relocating for the company so often in those twenty-six years. I acknowledged that her divisions had always delivered results and met expectations quarter over quarter, regardless of the economy or the circumstances.

But what I wanted to know from Sharon, who had indeed been outwardly supportive of Dan's integration into the division, was what kind of internal conversations she might be having about Dan. When I asked Sharon if she had tried to mentor Dan, she said, "Oh yes! He's just not coachable!" I gently asked a few more questions about her interactions, and a pattern emerged. Sharon's real opinion about Dan in any interaction she had with him came down to this: "Dan is an idiot, and he doesn't get it."

That sounded so much like my own story when I was a CPA. Everyone was an idiot, especially my boss – except for me! But before I even shared that story with Sharon, she saw it for herself. She had a sudden realization that she had been highly judgmental about everything Dan did since day one. She had thought some things about Dan that, if she had said them out loud, would have required a sincere apology to everyone within hearing distance.

But, Sharon did not like the idea that she might have to apologize. She said that as a female executive, she was tired of being the one to always apologize. She said she was not willing to demean herself by making apologies to Dan, regardless of her own poor performance as a business partner.

Seen from this perspective, it becomes clear why Dan – or anyone – might have been reluctant to really engage with Sharon in such an adversarial climate. Even Sharon could see why Dan had become withdrawn from her and had stopped connecting with her. Even though their offices were on the same hall, she and Dan had not talked face-to-face in six months.

As Sharon and I talked, I asked her some more questions about what kind of contributions Dan had made. Had his team had any success meeting their sales goals? It turned out they had met their baseline goals, but not really exceeded them in a way that would earn bonuses for the division. I pointed out that a team who meets their baseline goals is something to be grateful for. How much worse would it be if they could not even make their minimums?

Sharon laughed and had to admit that was true. With questions like this, we found several things Sharon could be grateful for in this situation – several ways Dan had been a success, not the total failure she had come to me about. From this position of gratitude, Sharon realized for herself that as long as she blamed Dan, she was sabotaging any hope of progress or success with her division.

Whatever evidence she might have to prove the guilt for the division's poor performance belonged to Dan's department, she could no longer afford the luxury of playing the victim. As long as she harbored this bitterly judgmental attitude instead of gratitude, she and her division would suffer. That is when Sharon aligned her attitude with her vision of success and took total responsibility for the situation.

Letting go of all the negative judgments about Dan, Sharon reached out to him across the chasm of silence that had grown between them. She met with Dan face-to-face. First, she acknowledged Dan for the results he and his team had achieved. Then, in a gentle but fearlessly honest way, she confessed and apologized for all her preconceived judgments about him. She shared all the reasons she had not been more supportive of him as a new leader. She admitted that the lack of collaboration and cooperation was entirely her responsibility. She took responsibility for the total lack of communication for the past six months. Sharon said, "Dan, I want to do whatever it takes to clean this up and earn your trust. I want us to work together to get our division turned around."

I should say that this gush of forthrightness shocked Dan at first. As you can imagine, Dan was surprised, and at first he hesitated to believe what he was hearing. Trust does not happen in an instant. We build it over time. In the days and weeks that followed, Sharon would earn that trust through her actions. And when she proved she was ready to be authentic, vulnerable, and candid with Dan, it invited him to open up to her about where he really did need some help. As Sharon demonstrated her dedication to taking full responsibility, Dan was inspired to see where he could take responsibility for his role in their lack of success.

This is the kind of genuine dialogue that you find in companies working to achieve total alignment. Sharon and Dan, in a matter of weeks, turned from bitter enemies into two strong collaborators working on the same team, towards the same goal of mutual success. They went from not speaking for half a year to daily meetings where they brainstormed great ideas for turning Dan's department and the entire division around.

A few months later, in the wake of the success they generated together, Sharon received an outstanding promotion and moved to a job she would enjoy until her retirement five years later. And do you know what? The division she helped transform kept on enjoying a high level of success year after year, long after she had moved on. She never did file that lawsuit.

This story should make clear the need to manage our responses, to manage our attitudes that make us react instead of respond, and the importance of fundamental self-leadership practices in getting your whole team aligned. Reactions tend to break down our connections with each other, to limit our ability to cooperate and collaborate. Reactions keep us feeling unsteady and unsafe. Reactions will poison our organization and keep us out of alignment with our values and vision. But, responding thoughtfully from a position of gratitude and acknowledgment, with personal responsibility and vulnerability, begins the conversations that build alignment with our colleagues, with our teams, and eventually throughout the entire organization, from top to bottom.

**React or Respond Self Test**

To get a sense of your own tendencies towards reacting or responding, honestly answer the brief questions in the following assessment.

### *React or Respond Self-Test*

Answer True or False based on what <u>other</u> people would say about you:

_____  1. When expectations are not met, I look to myself for responsibility.

_____  2. When preparing to communicate and clarify expectations, I consistently take time to prepare and script out the message.

_____  3. I routinely take think time to assess our situation and reflect on patterns and trends.

_____  4. I never rush or hurry. I am never late for meetings.

_____  5. I always have enough time between meetings to both document the results of the previous meeting and prepare myself for the upcoming meeting.

_____  6. I don't have to rely on my memory because I have plans, goals, the process, and interim milestones well-documented and understood by every team member.

———— 7. My team delivers results on time and on budget.

———— 8. My team members speak up with concerns early and frequently. We use these opportunities to clarify our expectations and brainstorm solutions.

———— 9. When breakdowns occur, I respond by pulling the team together to dissect the situation, identify corrective action, and document the lessons learned for future use.

———— 10. My peers view me as a role model for how to respond, rather than react. They do not see me putting out fires all day.

| If you responded True to... | Then you are... |
| --- | --- |
| All 10 Statements | An EXPERT at responding, not reacting. |
| 8-9 Statements | A PRO who is masterful at creating an environment of transparency and trust. |
| 5-7 Statements | ABOVE AVERAGE and could benefit from a more thoughtful, reflective approach to preparing your responses. |

| | |
|---|---|
| 3-4 Statements | A NOVICE at responding. You most likely react more often than respond, which causes you to be unpredictable and inconsistent. |
| Fewer than 3 Statements | A REACTOR who is training others to react rather than respond. Fire drills and the challenge of the day constantly require you to roll up your sleeves and be the hero. |

## Questions for Your Think Time

In a difficult situation I currently face, what can I find to be grateful for? What else in my life do I have to be grateful for in this moment?

Who on my team needs to be acknowledged for some unrecognized success? How did this success move us closer to realizing our vision? How can I express my appreciation in an acknowledgment? When might I do this in a public setting?

If I have a conflict currently, what does the other person need to be acknowledged for? Where have they succeeded, and how do they support our team?

Is my pace too fast? Would the people on my team agree with my answer?

What day this week can I schedule an hour of completely uninterrupted time to think and reflect on the challenges I face? When can I schedule this hour every week?

What are some situations that really touch a nerve with me? How do I react? How can I manage those situations with a more thoughtful response?

**Call to Action**

I commit to take the following actions by this date_____ in order to build a strong foundation of self-leadership in my actions and attitudes. I am doing these things not just for myself, but so I can bring my best self to my loved ones, my team, and my community.

1. _____

2. _____

3. _____

## CHAPTER 4

# Aligning Your Teams through Honest Communication

AS I SHARED in the introduction, the source of my frustration in my CPA career boiled down to one central concern: I was not being authentic about my own strengths and my vision for life and my career. Ken Blanchard, author of *The One Minute Manager*, has influenced me for years by always going back to the source of great leadership. He says it starts with looking at *you* first and foremost. Only then can you share who you are and what you stand for. But in my case, I lacked the self-awareness to even understand my own my natural gifts and talents. I was like a hamster on a wheel, running faster and faster but never gaining any traction for all my efforts.

*Alignment for Success* aims to free you from that wheel of frustration. We have already discussed how self-leadership brings a more authentic awareness of your own personal values and vision. You may have already begun developing a healthy perspective as described by Dr. Neil M. Yeager, author of *The Career Doctor,* which depends on how much you feel the work you do is an appropriate match for your skills, interests, and goals – and to the extent these feelings are consistent with the needs of the organization. The next step is entering, as your authentic self, into honest conversations with your co-workers and teams. *Alignment for Success* will guide you through this process, demonstrating the communication skills and style that will make these conversations effective at building alignment.

**What is Authenticity?**

Authenticity means living an authentic life. An authentic life is one where you know yourself. As quoted in the *Huffington Post* by Alena Hall, authenticity research pioneers Michael Kernis and Brian Goldman defined authenticity as "the unimpeded operation of one's true or core self in one's daily enterprise." When you are authentic, you know what your values are. You know your standards and expectations.

Because you know what your needs are, you know what works for you and what does not work for you. You can then align your life, your lifestyle, and your career with this awareness of your core values. Once you have the awareness to articulate to yourself who you truly are and what truly matters to you, you can prepare for honest conversations with your colleagues. Authenticity lays the foundation for these conversations that will bring your entire organization into alignment around a common vision and shared values.

Self-leadership gives us the means to manage the negative judgments and conversations we have in our heads on a daily basis. Self-leadership will steer us away from tendencies to be judgmental, defensive, and argumentative. But when we begin authentic conversations with our teams, we venture into emotional territory that may be scary for us at first. After all, complete authenticity requires us to be vulnerable. We must be willing to share openly and honestly about our strengths as well as our challenges and shortcomings. It may be uncomfortable or unfamiliar at first. But if we do not model the behaviors that build total alignment, then who will? *Alignment for Success* will coach you through developing yourself as a role model – a leader who can exemplify, through communication, the level of self-awareness and authenticity that will eventually align the entire organization.

## What is Honest Communication?

Honest communication is conveying ideas and discussing concerns in a manner that brings forth a variety of stakeholders' unique perspectives. Moreover, honest communication is based on the facts – not just a person's perspective. Perspective can often be formulated without proper context. Honest communication requires that we own our experiences and perspectives and share these in ways that invite others to feel confident in sharing theirs openly and honestly.

Honest communication requires sharing the proper context with everyone. Context includes both the history of the situation, "How did we get here today?" and the current goals and objectives. In other words, context provides the big picture.

Instead of saying, "I need your analysis of this situation by tomorrow at noon," you might consider more specifics such as, "Joe, as you know, I meet with the Board's finance committee on Thursday to review in more detail our proposal to expand our operations in Iowa. If I can get your analysis by Tuesday at noon, I'll have enough time to both read and reflect on your recommendations. That way, I can be fully prepared to present your analysis as well as share my own thoughts. As you and I have discussed, this expansion into Iowa is critical to getting our costs down."

Now, your colleague has the big picture. He understands why this deadline and his thorough analysis are so important. By taking the time to invest in his understanding, you show respect. You build more a more trusting relationship with him, and he feels empowered by understanding the big picture.

If authenticity is a state of being, then honest communication is an action we take based on that state of being. Honest communication grows out of authenticity. Our ability to foster authenticity among others is directly correlated with our ability to be authentic ourselves. It is not enough to simply know our self. As leaders, we must look for opportunities every day to *demonstrate* that we know ourselves. In order to leverage our personal success, we must share stories that illustrate how success came about when we aligned our actions with our values, strengths, and beliefs. These stories form much of the content of honest communication.

Many times, we avoid honest communication. We fear that speaking the truth about how we feel will only lead to conflict. Because no one enjoys conflict, we deny the reality of the situation or sweep it under the rug. Sometimes we even lie to ourselves about the seriousness of the situation. However, it is far more effective to address difficult situations at the first warning signs, through honest communication, before conflict has a chance to escalate.

This fear of conflict dissipates when we develop some structure for our honest communications. Just because we are authentic does not mean we can enter into potentially sensitive conversations without a plan. Our side of the conversation requires us to manage our initial attitude, what we offer the other person involved, and how we get them to engage with us from an authentic perspective. When preparing to engage in honest communication, keep these three elements in mind:

Step 1          Assume the other parties involved are innocent, and suspend all judgments.

Step 2          Acknowledge all successes, large and small, of the
                parties involved.
Step 3          Ask questions with curiosity and fascination, and
                listen closely to the answers.

Let us cover each one of these elements in more detail, since they are so fundamentally important to having the honest conversations that will build alignment.

**Step 1: Assume innocence**. Assume innocence on the part of others and take responsibility yourself.   If we assume guilt of others, we listen for evidence of their guilt.   If we assume innocence, then we listen for evidence of their innocence.   Remember the importance of managing our attitude.   If we have already taken personal responsibility as part of our commitment to self-leadership, we do not need to seek guilt or blame in others. It is that simple. When we accuse people, they get defensive, and communication breaks down. If we drop that judgmental attitude, we create an environment of safety where people feel comfortable telling us the straight scoop. If they feel supported no matter what they say, we will get to the truth of the matter with far less struggle.

**Step 2: Acknowledge successes.** An acknowledgment of others' successes reinforces expectations, recognizes accomplishment, and can even publicly affirm your colleagues. More importantly, acknowledgments create a positive attitude. Your colleagues will pay more attention, take more initiative, and come to the conversation with potential solutions. The second step reinforces the experience of safety that nurtures honest communication.

**Step 3: Ask questions.** The person who asks the questions is the person providing the leadership. But, keep in mind the importance of taking think time to prepare your questions thoughtfully.

The point is not to stun your team with a barrage of questions. You do not want to be perceived as an interrogator or a bully as you make your inquiries. The goal is to use questions as the basis for a thoughtful discussion where we identify our shared goals, potential solutions to conflict, and a mutual understanding.

## Staying in the Conversation

Honest communication means staying in these conversations long enough to hear and validate everyone's perspective and experiences. Too often, decision-making processes are based on the squeaky wheel getting the grease. But, allowing those squeaky wheels on our teams to dominate all our meetings and conversations often means ignoring some very important perspectives from less vocal, less outgoing team members. Hearing everyone's thoughts on a project brings out a broad range of perspectives, concerns, and potential unintended consequences. This degree of sharing and discussion will often identify, in advance, the risk of potential failures. Honest communication is a fully inclusive process where the conversation does not end until everyone has had a chance to speak and be heard – even the most cautious and reserved members of the team.

The importance of this inclusive communication became clear in the wake of BP's 2010 oil spill in the Gulf of Mexico. The worst oil spill in history will damage the ecosystem for decades to come. In January, 2011, the White House's Oil Spill Commission released their report detailing the faults that led to the spill. John Broder reported in *The New York Times* that the Commission offered this summary of the causes in terms of management:

> "Better management of decision-making processes within BP and other companies, better communication within and between BP and its contractors, and effective

training of key engineering and rig personnel would have prevented the Macondo incident."

James Dupree, President for BP's US Gulf of Mexico business, promised to increase communication with all the people these disasters affect. Emran Hussain's 2011 article for *Arabian Oil and Gas* quoted Dupree:

> "Last autumn, we made an ongoing commitment to share what we have learned and the experience we gained during the Deepwater Horizon incident response with the world... We have shared our insights with regulators, participated in public forums, worked directly with industry bodies, and published our lessons learned."

These leaders may have finally gotten the message: honest communication based on awareness and authenticity can prevent disasters like the oil spill. It can prevent the resulting devastation to our economy, our environment, and our culture.

## Honest Communication is Not about Forcing Outcomes

Honest communication is not compelling others through forcefulness. It is not brashly sharing your judgments and assessments. These approaches tear down trust, respect, openness, and all sense of safety. When we speak harshly or forget to consider the other person's perspective, we drive out any possibility of trust. Force and intensity drive our alignment and usher in fear.

This is why *Alignment for Success* focuses so much more on sharing instead of forcing. Honest communication means speaking openly about what is working for you and what is not working. To achieve an environment where everyone feels comfortable speaking honestly, we must be the first to step up and model this behavior. Rather than accuse, we share. Rather than force, we listen.

But, this gentle approach does not mean we can ignore real problems or sweep them under the rug. Honest communication is not about being nice in a shallow way to avoid hurting anyone's feelings. Instead, honest communication is the process by which we address the core concerns in an effective way. We want to uncover root causes through identifying what works, as in acknowledgments, followed by an open discussion where our people can identify what is not working. Only then can the team collaborate on solutions to what troubles us. In this way, we nurture an environment where innovative solutions naturally grow out of honest conversations, rather than using intimidation and force to bludgeon our teams into innovation. The latter approach may sometimes appear get the job done, but it builds resentment – not alignment.

## Results of Honest Communication

Honest communication results in decisions based on facts. By taking into account everyone's unique perspective, we discover potential unintended consequences of the decisions we face. Because everyone on the team has a chance to be heard, they feel commitment to the resulting decision. This is true of not just our colleagues and co-workers but our customers as well. When everyone who has a stake in the decision has a say, the resulting decisions become much more aligned with the total organization – from customer to frontline worker, from upper management to the CEO, from the Board of Directors to the shareholders.

Without this degree of alignment, you risk sabotage. Sabotage will come from those people who not only did not support the decision but never even felt like they had a say in the matter. Sadly, this sabotage happens every day in some organizations. This sabotage is not necessarily a dramatic Hollywood-style act of espionage. It is the disgruntled worker who milks the clock. It is the colleague who goes behind your back to send whole departments on missions that directly undermine the decision we thought we all agreed to. It is the utter indifference to inefficient processes that could be made better, if only people considered the "suggestion box" as something other than a cruel joke. It is the customers who do not think anyone is listening, so they leave.

Sabotage takes many forms, but honest communication will prevent it. When people get their voices heard, when we recognize and acknowledge their perspectives, they have less motivation to resort to resentful acts of sabotage. They know that someone actually cares.

When teams communicate with honesty and authenticity, people feel more confident about their roles, the direction of the company, and the value they bring it every day. When people feel valued as key members of a team, they will step up, take even greater initiative and ownership of their challenges, and begin generating amazing results. When they become clear on the vision you share with them, when they know what is expected of them and that they will be recognized for meeting that expectation, everything they do begins to align with the vision.

Innovation thrives in a fully aligned environment like this. When people feel confident about success, they feel comfortable reaching outside their own comfort zones. Our comfort zones support us in playing small, in being cautious and overly prudent. Honest communication creates environments where fear dissipates, and team members demonstrate a willingness to take measured risks. They will bravely push the envelope, experimenting with new and different approaches that lead to innovative solutions, new products, and game-changing ideas.

A company called Pool Covers in Fairfield, CA demonstrates the effectiveness of these inclusive conversations and communal decision-making processes. Like the other 83 percent of INC's 2010 Top Small Company Workplaces, Pool Covers opens their books to their employees. In addition, new employees receive training to qualify for the employee stock ownership program. Leigh Buchanan reported for Inc. in *Opening the Books and Motivating Workers* that after being trained, new hires at Pool Covers "spend four or five days digging into the company's financials." These new employees then "collaborate on an idea for improving the company's bottom line... CEO Claire King marvels at her new hires' ingenuity."

Buchanan reports on another winner, Ginger Bay Salon and Spa in Kirkwood, MO, who displays financials "prominently on a scoreboard in the break room... The board announces each employee's daily sales results and whether he or she met their goals... 'Behavior changed overnight,' says Laura Ortmann, co-owner of the Salon. 'No one wants their name next to a low number.'"

How do workers respond? "'I love numbers, and I love knowing how I'm doing,' says nail technician Terri Kavanagh. 'Laura uses the term "financial fitness," and she's right. It's just like working out. Once you get your muscles toned, you can perform at a higher level.'" When production goals are clearly defined and publicly posted, people will work hard to beat the daily goals.

Because of these small business owners' willingness to be authentic and vulnerable, they built extremely high degrees of alignment. By taking responsibility for articulating their expectations clearly and consistently, they paved the way for their people to step up and bring real value to the company. Why? Because people naturally want to be successful.

My 40-plus years of experience tell me that pay raises only motivate people for two to three pay cycles before they tend to forget that they received a raise. Some companies invest a lot of money in building cafeterias and fully-stocked break rooms with ping-pong tables and pool tables. These material incentives are all well and good. However, I consistently find that people are motivated by success. When they have a voice in decisions and understand their role in achieving the vision, when honest communication has assured them of the resources they need to succeed, and when they have collaborated to build the structures they need to succeed, they will move heaven and earth on a daily basis to make success happen. This is why a fully aligned organization succeeds.

## A Role Model for Honest Communication

Kathy, the Chief Marketing Officer of a national magazine, was in a meeting with her peers and with Robert, the CEO of the company. They met to review the results of the employee satisfaction survey. Robert seemed disappointed that their scores had actually gone down over the past year. He was especially concerned about the low scores related to the opinions of his direct reports – the people in this meeting. All of his direct reports felt strongly that Robert did not trust their decision-making abilities and therefore would not delegate making decisions to them. They know these scores reflect this frustration.

Kathy spent the first part of the meeting wondering if she should fight this battle. She knew Robert could be so obstinate about his abilities that he came across as arrogant. She knew too well of his tendency to swoop down on an already chaotic situation and make it worse by intimidating his workers. She knew he was this way largely because he had relied on his aggressive style to get things done for thirty-five years

But, Kathy also cared for the 300 people in her division and the price they paid for Robert's aggressive style. The stress led to low productivity from disgruntled workers coupled with high turnover as people fled the toxic environment Robert created. The chaos and fear had taken a toll on Kathy's division for too long. How could she use honest communication to enter into a productive dialogue with Robert, instead of meeting him head-on for yet another conflict?

Twenty minutes into the meeting, Kathy finally spoke up. She said, "Bob, you seem to prefer to control decision-making at your level. I know you are most comfortable with this approach. Frankly, we have enjoyed a lot of success in the past because of your smarts. However, as our company enters this growth mode, I would like to see you authorize each one of us to also make our own decisions. With enough context and guidelines, each of us can be trusted. But the way it is now, I feel like I have to come to you with every single decision – big or small."

Emboldened by Kathy's honesty about her feelings and her acknowledgment of Robert's success, the rest of the team slowly chimed in. Each of them had many experiences where they developed the same feeling that they had to bring Robert each and every decision. Robert sat back and listened thoughtfully as the team shared the consequences of his controlling style.

Kathy feared she had opened the floodgates for conflict by speaking authentically. But, when she approached Robert later that day to apologize for her candor, she found out how grateful he was that she spoke up. Robert acknowledged her by saying, "Kathy, I can count on you to always tell me the truth."

In the days and weeks that followed, they developed a much stronger connection based on trust and respect. As Robert learned to relax his grip on the reins of the company, his senior leaders began to step up in powerful ways. Empowered to make their own decisions, they began eliminating the cost of fear and chaos in their own departments with innovative strategies.

And, as Robert and his senior team opened their doors to honest communication, they inspired a management culture that spread throughout the company. Did Robert get those improved scores he wanted so badly on the next employee satisfaction improve? You bet he did – and Kathy's initiative in authentic and honest conversation paved the way for that success.

## Language that Creates Safe Environments

Creating a culture of high performance starts with creating an environment where everyone feels safe to say *everything*. Building an environment of trust depends to a great degree on the language we choose for our responses and questions. At the Halpin Companies, we call choosing the right language "throwing others the ball in a way they can catch it."

Early in our history, one of our clients shared a story with us about coaching his third-grade son's basketball team. He said that when a teammate does not catch a basketball thrown to them, he does not coach the one that dropped the ball. He goes back to the child who threw the ball. In his most patient, coach-like voice, he asks, "Did you maybe throw that ball too hard? Do you think it might have been too high?" This approach created an environment of safety for those that couldn't catch the ball. Even more importantly, he was instilling a sense of personal responsibility on the part of the child who threw the ball.

To create a safe space where everyone feels comfortable speaking authentically to each other, use language like the examples that follow. Ask questions and listen closely to the answers. Keep going deeper without providing solutions, so your people have a chance to speak.

"This doesn't work for me. What would work for me is…"

"What would it take for you to be able to…"

"I know that the rest of the team would like to know this. Will you tell them, or do you want me to tell them?

"This is important to me, and I can't give it the full attention it deserves right now. Can we set a time to meet later when I can focus on this conversation?"

"My recollection is different than this. Help me recall…."

"I'm confused. Help me understand this."

"Tell me what that means for you"

If conflict arises, use language such as, "I am so sorry that I have allowed this situation to occur. I am going to do whatever it takes to clean this up and regain your trust."

**Questions for Your Think Time**

With whom do I need to have an honest conversation? What are the contributions and successes I can acknowledge them for?

Can I think of some situations where I tried to force an outcome instead of opening a dialogue about it? How could I have handled that differently with honest communication?

Can I think of some situations that currently have me worried, angry, or upset? Who do I blame for these situations?

In a situation where I currently blame others, what actions or inaction of mine have contributed to the conflict? What must I do to take full responsibility for how this turns out?

On my team, what is on everyone's mind that everyone is afraid to talk about? How can I open a dialogue by sharing my own concerns about that?

Who on my team is afraid to speak up? Who is afraid to speak to me personally about their concerns? What can I do to begin honestly communicating with these people?

What do I need to do in my program of self-care to give me the support I need to have these conversations and build strong alignment?

**Call to Action**

I commit to taking the following three actions by this date_____
to develop honest communication on my team and in my organization.   I am doing these things not just for myself, but to bring my
best self to my loved ones, my team, and my community.

1. _____

2. _____

3. _____

## CHAPTER 5

# Aligning Your
# Organization Everywhere You Go

THERE ARE UNLIMITED opportunities to cascade alignment down into and across an organization. Every encounter with another person provides an opportunity to foster a stronger connection. Every email to a team, group, or division provides another opportunity to send consistent, empowering messages. Board decisions and actions provide an opportunity to clarify the long-term strategic vision for the organization. Every team meeting, every performance appraisal, every act of honest communication provides the opportunity to further articulate and clarify expectations and standards.

Every encounter is an opportunity to either build trust. Every conversation is an opportunity to acknowledge others, to demonstrate that you appreciate another person, and that you have a commitment to align their roles with their strengths. Every failure is an opportunity for leadership to demonstrate their commitment to innovation by affirming every lesson learned – even the costly ones.

The question is: Are we willing to use every opportunity to engage others more effectively?

## Aligning Roles and Strengths

To understand what it means to have people in roles that align with their strengths, consider the story of Barbara. Barbara came to us about the challenges she faced as director over 250 claims processors at division of a global insurance company. While her well-respected company had enjoyed sizeable market share for many years, Barbara had lately been so stressed that she could not even sleep through the night. Her department churned out thousands of claims every week. But something had started to go terribly wrong. Customers were leaving in frustration. The efficiency of the claims department had plummeted. Her workers had begun abusing the company's leave policies. Conversations around the water cooler had taken a turn for the worse, generating an atmosphere of ugliness and frustration. Nothing was getting done. Or, if it did get done, it got done all wrong. Supervisors spent countless hours doing needless re-work of the same claims due to the high error rate of the staff. Barbara wanted to know if we could help.

I began by acknowledging Barbara for her commitment to turning this situation around. I acknowledged her for committing to find the right tools and methods to bring success back to her team. I acknowledged the courage it took to admit to her feelings of powerlessness and frustration. And then, I told her about the assessments we use at The Halpin Companies.

We helped Barbara understand her team members' strengths with an assessment developed by Lynn Taylor, founder of Taylor Protocols, called the Core Values Index™. We have used it extensively with our clients for four years. With this assessment, Barbara and her supervisors got very useful data on all 250 claims processors. We identified their top performers with easy questions like, "Who on your team can you rely on for answers when you get stumped?"

And most importantly, we identified the strengths and values of every single person in her division.

By using scientific assessments, Barbara identified her fifty poorest performers. But, because we had identified their strengths, she could find other departments in the company where they would excel at their jobs. Only a handful of this group had to be let go.

But, do you know what is interesting about that handful of people? They still send Barbara pictures and postcards. They thank her for having the courage to tell them the truth. Once they got a chance to examine their core values and their unique strengths, they found things in life they really enjoy. Some of them no longer work in corporate America at all. They became dog walkers, forest rangers, and small business owners. One owns a day care service where she provides for the children of her former co-workers.

These personal successes happened alongside some stunning bottom-line events at the company. Barbara's payroll expense decreased from over $10 million annually to just under $7 million. When we helped her get the right people in the right roles doing the right thing, the company found themselves with a smaller department of 175 claims processors who exceeded Barbara's wildest expectations. Barbara's department realized a productivity increase of over 300 percent in the coming year.

The effect of this powerfully aligned team spread throughout the company, from the customers to the executive suite. Policyholders were thrilled to see their claims paid quickly and accurately now. The claims processors enjoyed tremendous recognition and bonuses for their results. The negative atmosphere vanished, and management became free to manage instead of put out fires all day. The company's executives delighted in the improvements to the bottom line. The shareholders of the company expressed their appreciation by lifting the share price and increasing the market capitalization. That is what alignment looks like in action: people in roles that align with their strengths.

## Alignment at the Executive Level

Barbara's story illustrates alignment on a department-wide scale. But, aligning even one person can have just as profound an effect on an organization. Consider Nathan's story, where all the elements of taking think time, slowing down, giving acknowledgments, and having honest communication came together to turn distress into success.

Nathan was once the Chief Operating Officer of a manufacturing organization with almost 10,000 employees. Most people perceived him as an extremely effective leader. He had risen from a front-line engineering role through almost a dozen layers of management before his last promotion to COO. He took pride in understanding the inner workings of the company.

But, parts of Nathan's organization had suffered. Nathan had seven functional areas he held accountability for. Unfortunately, he only focused his time and attention on four. He gave his attention to the four where he had previously worked, neglecting the important areas of finance, human resources, and information technology. While appearing supportive and friendly to these areas on the outside, Nathan consistently delayed any support for these functions. He planted seeds of doubt. He stalled. He caused the entire leadership team to delay decisions that would have provided additional support.

His inauthentic behavior negatively affected the success of the administrative leaders in these departments. That frustration led to high turnover at their highest levels. Nathan's outward friendliness to their endeavors kept them from seeing the reality of his obstructive behavior.

Fortunately, Roger, the CEO, started to see the turnover trends and connected the dots. Upon reflection, he realized Nathan was not supporting his administrative leaders. Roger saw clearly, for the first time, that Nathan's narrow focus left the administrative leaders neglected and abandoned.

Roger took time to script out a conversation with Nathan. He did not want to put Nathan on the defensive or break down their trusting relationship. But, Roger knew that Nathan's performance put the entire company at risk. Roger's deep commitment to creating a win/win prompted him to slow down and take three whole weeks to reflect on the situation, thoughtfully scripting his questions for Nathan.

He also looked for just the right time to meet. Roger knew that if Nathan was rushed, fatigued from travel, or overwhelmed in any way, then he would be less likely to engage in an empowering, productive way. When Roger found just the right time, he was prepared. He felt confident they could resolve this and still maintain the respect they had built in ten years of working together.

Roger started the conversation with an acknowledgment of Nathan. He shared that he had never experienced a leader more effective in delivering results through their people and still having those direct reports feel as if their leader was also their best ally and friend. Roger shared a specific example of one of Nathan's key reports delivering a solution in a more comprehensive and timely manner than Roger had even hoped for. He noticed a glow on Nathan's face that let him know Nathan felt good about himself and his results.

Then, Roger started to ask a few questions, one at a time, giving Nathan a chance to think them over. "Did you notice the recent trend in turnover among your direct reports? Do you have a sense of the real reasons, not just the surface reasons, why these key people left? Do you realize that the trend related only to administrative, not operational or service-line, leaders?"

From this gentle, yet purposeful discussion, Nathan started to see what Roger had already seen. When nudged, Nathan realized he had unintentionally sabotaged his own direct reports. He knew he could no longer afford the luxury of focusing only on the goals and needs of operational leaders. Nathan was embarrassed and ashamed of himself.

Fortunately, Roger valued Nathan and would not allow him to beat himself up. Roger reinforced, through additional acknowledgments of Nathan's recent successes, all the value Nathan brought to their enterprise. Roger had learned, over the years, that if a person was unsuccessful, it usually boiled down to one of three reasons. They either did not have a commitment to the goal, the skills to reach the goal, or the structure they needed to reach it. Roger took responsibility for creating this structure for Nathan.

Nathan needed to go individually and then collectively to his administrative leaders. Roger coached Nathan to take full responsibility for their lack of success and to share a commitment to do whatever was necessary to help them be successful. Roger and Nathan agreed to meet and brainstorm ideas for structures that would help Nathan build stronger connections, fully share his people's commitments, and understand what resources they needed for their projects.

Where is Nathan now? Roger promoted him to be CEO of his own subsidiary, but with a smaller staff. Once Roger became aware of both Nathan's strengths and his limitations, it was easy to align his role with his strengths. The subsidiary had far fewer people than Nathan's old department, which gave him an opportunity to support everyone on his teams instead of being overwhelmed and showing favoritism. At the subsidiary, each department gets the necessary attention and resources they need from Nathan. By proving to Roger that he could support everyone, not just his favorite departments, Nathan proved he could truly lead his own organization.

**Build Trust and Connect with Others**
Arkadi Kulmann was the Chairman and CEO of ING Direct, at one time the largest online bank in North America. He believes in what he calls "emotional vulnerability" as the driver to building trust and connections among team members. He often speaks to the MBA students at the Richard Ivey School of Business at the University of Western Ontario and has published case studies for Ivey Publishing. As a follower of Mr. Kulmann, I've learned what I believe are his secrets to building a transparent, aligned executive team. He often speaks of the importance of celebrating successes together, yet also about sharing times we did not succeed so well in life and in business. Though some feel shame for failures, he believes risking failure builds character, and seeks to build the risk of failure into teams.

For example, the marketing team at ING Direct faced the challenge of marketing a new kind of banking service. They boldly experimented with many approaches. Since their target market was a tech-savvy professional, they certainly invested in building an online presence. But, they also experimented with old-fashioned advertising. They bought ad space on billboards and bus stops, using signs with creative messages to attract attention. They took risks to reach their target market using both old and new approaches, without knowing which ones would fail and which would succeed.

How do leaders create these environments where people are comfortable taking risks? I worked with one CEO who showed remarkable abilities in this area. She took the time to get to know her people first as *people* with a life outside of work. Once she established those personal connections, she took the time to identify and acknowledge their successes.

She routinely tours her company's facilities, including times on weekends or late at night so she can meet everyone on every shift. During these tours, she shares stories about the recent successes her people have enjoyed. She knows her people will probably not remember her slideshow presentations, but they will definitely remember the stories of one of their co-workers who went the extra mile, or a story about an incredibly happy customer. All her interactions with her people, from the top of the company on down, reinforce this experience of sharing and communication – of trust.

## Conduct Experiments

Bill George, the former CEO of Medtronics, demonstrated a similar commitment to leading by walking around – to demonstrating his commitment to trust and alignment by interacting with his people. He spoke frankly and honestly about his concerns by sharing personal stories of his own failures and what he learned from them. He was the first to take personal responsibility and never played the game of blaming others when things went wrong. He invited every employee to voice their concerns about even the slightest potential design flaw.

Thanks to his encouragement, his teams uncovered every possible potential failure – and then brainstormed ways to prevent those failures. In the Medtronics philosophy, they believed in building systems to identify and prevent failures. As a result, people never failed. Only the systems failed. By framing failures in this light, Medtronics removed fear and ushered in an era of bold innovation.

This type of culture exemplifies my belief that we need to conduct experiments, and that we can only do so when our people are not afraid to fail. After all, a scientist looks at a failed experiment as a source of data. Why did it fail? What does that teach us? How could we improve our experimental design to get closer to success next time?

This scientific perspective on experiments puts the focus on learning. In *The Inner Game of Work*, Timothy Gallwey shares a concept that I use every day. We must adopt an attitude that we are in the greatest seminar on Earth. This seminar is called "My Life." We must maintain this attitude to learn all the lessons we need to learn to fully succeed. An organization that can experiment can also innovate and grow. Without the freedom to experiment, no one will feel safe enough to take even a small risk. Without risk, we do not evolve, we do not grow. Without growth, our organizations cannot evolve and flourish.

When scientists conduct an experiment, they collect data. They analyze the data and draw conclusions. From these conclusions, they form a theory or a model that can make predictions. Then, they conduct more experiments to prove or disprove the theory. All the while, scientists know they are moving forward. Even when the experiment turns out other than how they expected, they have gained greater awareness of the situation and all the variables that affect the outcome.

Judging themselves or their colleagues for any shortcomings in the experiment has no place in this scientific perspective. Instead, scientists keep experimenting until they discover the formula for a successful outcome. In the same way, an organization that builds total alignment knows both the freedom from fear and the freedom to experiment. This leads to unparalleled levels of innovation.

## Taking Success Step by Step

We believe that openness and honesty make for the best relationships because they lead to trust. We value strong relationships with everyone who has a stake in our organization: managers, direct reports, customers, vendors, business partners, team members, and co-workers. Strong, positive relationships that are open and honest are a big part of what differentiates a fully aligned company from the others. Strong relationships allow us to accomplish much more than we would be able to otherwise.

Strong relationships involve developing emotional connections. Always act with integrity in your relationships. Be compassionate, friendly, and loyal. At the end of the day, what you say and do matter less than how you make people feel. People feel good about relationships where they know someone truly cares about them, both personally and professionally. As we work together to build alignment in ourselves, our teams, and our entire organization, a focus on communication will help everyone understand how their daily activities connect to the big picture and express the vision.

*Alignment for Success* has provided you with a road map to implement, within hours, the steps to build self-leadership, engage in honest communication, clarify the vision and what it means for your team, and build alignment throughout your organization. Taken step-by-step, these practical tools of self-leadership and communication will transform your life and take your company to the next level of success. We encourage you to start today.

**Questions for Your Think Time**

Who on my team is in a role that perfectly aligns with their strengths, beliefs, and values? Who is not?

What instruments are we currently using to assess the strengths of everyone in our organization? Can we improve them?

Who on my team is incredibly effective at building relationships with others? What can I learn from their methods and style?

Of the five people I interact with most on a daily basis, how would I rate the strength of our connection with each other? Do some of these connections need improvement where trust is concerned?

Do people in my organization feel secure enough to conduct experiments and try new solutions? If not, what fears are holding them back? What can I do to relieve those fears?

What gains have I seen so far from my program of self-care and self-leadership?

What are the three most important concepts I have learned by reading *Alignment for Success*?

**Call to Action**

I commit to taking the following actions by _____ to understand the strengths of everyone on my team, and make sure their role aligns with those strengths. I am doing these things not just for myself, but to bring out the best in my people for the sake of their loved ones, their teams, and our communities.

1. _____

2. _____

3. _____

# Works Cited

Breen, Bill. "The Clear Leader." *Fast Company*. 1 Mar. 2005.

Broder, John M. "Blunder Abounded Before Spill, Panel Says." *New York Times*. 5 Jan 2011.

Buchanan, Leigh. "Opening the Books and Motivating Workers: How Companies Such as Pool Covers and Ginger Bay Salon & Spa Use Open-book Management to Get the Best out of Their Employees." *Inc.* 8 Jun. 2010.

Collins, Tracy A. "One-on-one with Arianna Huffington." *Science of the Mind Magazine*. Jul. 2014.

Connors, Roger and Smith, Tom. *How Did That Happen? Holding People Accountable for Results the Positive, Principled Way.* New York: Penguin Group, 2009.

Connors, Roger, et al. *The Oz Principle: Getting Results through Individual and Organizational Accountability.* New York: Penguin Group, 2004.

Gallwey, W. Timothy. *The Inner Game of Work: Focus, Learning, Pleasure, and Mobility in the Workplace.* New York: Random House, 2000.

Hall, Alena. "6 Signs You're a Truly Genuine Person." *Huffington Post.* 29 Jul. 2014.

Hussain, Emran. "Interim Marine Well Containment System Launched." *Arabian Oil and Gas.* 22 Feb. 2011.

Shellenbarger, Sue. "Multitasking Makes You Stupid: Studies Show Pitfalls of Doing Too Much at Once." *Wall Street Journal.* 27 Feb. 2003.

# About the Author

 MOTIVATED BY A passion for success for everyone, Katharine Halpin makes contributions to the field of integrative thinking every day. She helps leaders focus on two opposing perspectives simultaneously: "What is best for the bottom line?" as well as "What is best for the team?"

Using The Halpin Companies' proven methods, organizations of all sizes have increased the value for their owners/shareholders, their customers and their industries by solving business problems quickly and strategically.

Katharine helps leaders:

- Clarify their Strategic Vision, the Mission & Shared Commitment,
- Align around the Vision and Plan in order to drive results strategically, and
- Get the right people driving the right results.

Katharine presents keynotes at regional and national conferences as well as in her client companies. Her seminars and leadership development programs focus on driving results by nurturing connections and building transparency at every level, in every interaction. She is a facilitator in the areas of innovation, change, and bringing out the best in others. The Halpin Companies' programs include:

Right People, Right Results, Right Now
Bring Out the Best in Others
Connecting Each Employee to Your Vision, Mission, and Strategy
Making Work Work for Everyone
Invest in Yourself and Your Team to Increase Your Company's
Value
Hard Way or the Easy Way? You Choose

Katharine is a member of Charter 100 of Phoenix, the American Institute of CPAs (AICPA,) the National Speakers Association (NSA,) and the International Coach Federation (ICF.) Katharine is one of only 674 professional around the globe that hold the designation of Master Certified Coach. Katharine was awarded this designation by the ICF in December, 1998.

**Katharine Halpin**
**The Halpin Companies, Inc.**
**1-888-48COACH**

**HalpinCompany.com**
**K.Halpin@HalpinCompany.com**